Accountant
Marketing Secrets:
Explosive Strategies to Instantly Improve Your Accounting
Business and Increase Your Income Fast

Social Media Marketing Series

A.J. Stone

ISBN-13:
978-1530897575

ISBN-10:
1530897572
:

CONTENTS

Contents

ACCOUNTANT MARKETING SECRETS

1 INTRODUCTION

Why are you reading this book?

Think about it for a second. What triggered you to take notice and select this book?

Were you curious about how it could help your business? Are you looking to make more money? Gain new customers? Or do you fall in one of the following categories?

- You are new to the accountant business and are not sure how to get customers.
- You have been following what other accountant business owners are doing without understanding why.
- You feel financial pressure closing in and need to do something quickly.
- You are marketing, but are not getting the results you expect.

Maybe you were under the impression that once you learned your craft, you would just put a sign on the door and people would flock to buy from you?

Wrong!

Learning how to become an accountant and running a business are two distinctly different things. Understanding this concept is critical if you want to have any successful business. There are people who go to college specifically to learn how to run and manage a business.

What if you don't have the time or interest to do the same, but you need your accountant business to be successful?

If you are reading this then you realize that you need a marketing strategy. At the very least, you realize that you need to gain more customers.

My job is to show you how effective the following marketing strategies can be in building your customer list. Your job is to understand the importance of marketing in your business.

If your goal is to make a living selling your craft, then you must believe that marketing your business is *more* important that what you are selling. Once you are a believer in the power of marketing, then you must take massive action consistently to implement these strategies every single day.

This book will show you how to use these strategies to increase sales, form a customer base and establish yourself as the premier accountant in your area.

Understanding the Value of Marketing Your Business

The biggest hurdle to overcome is realizing that you need to market yourself and learning how to do it so your prospects don't feel like they are being sold. I'm sure you can remember a time when someone has tried to sell you something. How did it make you feel? Did you recognize the sales pitch? Were you impressed when they did a good job? Did you feel awkward when they did a bad job?

Contrary to popular belief, it doesn't matter what you know. If you don't have anyone to sell your product or service to, you don't make money.

Before you can sell anything to anyone, you must learn how to get their attention. Not hitting them over the head with a sales pitch every time you run into them, or saturating your social media posts with self-promotion. The trick is to get their attention by showing an interest in them- not yourself. This is an art that can be learned relatively quickly.

There are two major parts to any business-- bringing in new business and managing existing business. When performed correctly, the majority of your time will be spent balancing both.

Bringing in new business

When you want prospects to become your customers you must go where they are. This means that you must be prepared to get social. If you tend to be introverted, you are going to have to step out of that shell a bit. It doesn't mean you have to be gung-ho Mr./Miss Personality and spent late nights at every community charity event and function, but it means you should be constantly on the lookout for opportunities to insert yourself into community events where you can mingle and network.

Fortunately, there are a variety of ways to do this which are discussed later (and many are agreeable with the introvert personality.)

Managing existing business

The other half of your business requires you to keep the customers you have content and satisfied with your performance. It is ten times less expensive to keep an existing client than it is to acquire a new one, so customer service is a huge consideration in your business.

This means that your time spent on this task will include consistent follow-up, feedback from customers on your performance and open communication. Your customers want to know their needs are being heard and met. When you do not return phone calls, or are unavailable for long periods of time, this can create serious doubt and uncertainty in them.

You must be willing to devote everything you have, everything it takes to give your customers a positive experience when doing business with you.

There are plenty of accountants to choose from, but your customers chose you. Don't make them sorry for doing so. Step up to the plate and be the best professional you can be by going above and beyond for them every time.

2 IT'S NOT ALL ABOUT YOU

One of the biggest mistakes business owners make is assuming that marketing means that the more information they can throw at prospects about themselves and/or their products and services, the simpler it will be to turn those prospects into customers.

This is one of the worst things you can do.

I'm sure you've heard the phrase, "no one cares how much you know until they know how much you care." This is undeniably true. Customers don't care about your accolades and accomplishments (at least not until they believe that you can help them with their needs.) Therefore, do not expect customers to be impressed with your experience until you directly connect with meeting their needs first.

A good place to start is to ask them what they believe their needs are. They may think they know, but sometimes they may not. That's why you are the professional. You can point out things they haven't thought about and advise them of the best course of action.

However, wait until you have let them thoroughly express what they believe their needs are. They need to feel heard and that you are listening to them. If they get the feeling in any way that you are just waiting for them to stop talking so you can start talking about yourself, you've lost them. They aren't going to trust you. They aren't going to feel confident that you know what they need and they definitely aren't going to be impressed with how much you know.

In this business, it's not all about you. In fact, none of it should be about you. It is all about the customer's needs and meeting those needs.

That is not to say that you should incur abuse, rudeness or disrespect from anyone. It means that you run your business as a professional with the intent on helping as many people as you can and knowing that your services are worthy of the commissions you make.

Help them first and the money will come.

3 THE RIGHT MINDSET

If your primary motivation entering the accountant business world was to make a lot of money then perhaps you should revise that intention to include more than monetary gain. Your trade is about helping people solve their problems. That's why they come to you and that is why you have a job. Your first goal should be to help people. When you make that a priority, the money will follow.

If you are desperate to make this month's bills or rent payment, your desperation will show through in how you interact with others. The last thing you need is for prospects or customers to think you have to make this commission. It does little to foster trust that you will do what is in their best interest instead of your own.

Instead, come to the situation with an attitude of generosity and helping your customers get what they need. This is a much better vibe to give off to others. It will build confidence that reinforces their decision to buy from you. Have you wondered why the harder you try to chase after customers, the more elusive they become? It could be because you were putting out a vibe of desperation that they picked up on. I know it can be stressful to have the bills piling up and wondering when the next paycheck is coming, but you make it harder when you focus on that instead of providing a quality customer service experience for your customers.

People want to do for others who do for them. All you have to do is stop trying to force it and change your attitude to one of giving. When you do this you will receive far greater than you give.

4 THE LAW OF RECIPROCITY

This entire book is centered on one crucial theme. It is the secret killer, the number one law of sales and marketing.

The Law of Reciprocity.

What does it mean?

Simply put, it means that you do or give something of value to someone else without expecting anything in return and you will find that human nature compels others to give back to you.

The term "value" can mean anything that is considered to have great importance. In our case, most of the time the valuable thing is free information.

Why would you want to give away something of value for free?

It builds trust and credibility in you as a professional. It reinforces your reputation that you are interested in meeting the needs of your customers and that you will put their needs above your own.

Giving away free information that helps your customers understand their problems and how to solve them builds you as a subject-matter expert in your field. In other words, they know where to go when they need information—you.

The Law of Reciprocity works in our lives for more than just business. How we treat others and how we make others feel is reflected in how they treat us. Someone having a bad day? Pour kindness into them, make them laugh and guaranteed they will remember, appreciate and help you when you need it.

The key is to truly not expect anything in return. Your goal should be to build a relationship with people, not try to sell them right on the spot. They already know you are a accountant. When the time comes for them to utilize your services, make them remember why they should call you first.

5 THREE SALES & MARKETING PRINCIPLES

1. Know your audience.

Who is your audience? Do you know? Beyond the gender and age demographics, you need to spend some time thinking about the answer to this question. Who do you want your audience to be?

No, the answer isn't "everyone." That's too broad. The key to a successful accountant business is drilling down to find your specialized niche. Certainly you will get referrals and one-off interests from those not in your niche, but your job is to seek out and find those who fit your key specialty.

So what should your niche be?

That depends. The goal to successful marketing is forming relationships. Usually relationships are built when common interests are shared, so it would stand to reason that you should seek out those who share similar interests as you do. For example, if you are a hobbyist, then seeking out others who share your interest can create an instant bond, whereas trying to appeal to a broad audience without knowing anything about their interest can waste a lot of your time marketing to the wrong people.

2. Know how to keep their interest first.

Make a list of all of your interests and hobbies. Then for each item, make a list of all possible ways you can find others who share your interests. Community events, clubs and online meeting sites are good places to start.

The good thing about starting with your own interests is that you already know the details, intricacies and terminology associated with them. When your interests are the same as your prospects, it is much easier to keep your prospects' interests first. It is easier to stay on track and have something to talk about.

Show your enthusiasm about the mutual interest you both share but be careful not to get too carried away. This isn't a contest to show them how much you know about the subject. It is an opportunity to get *them* talking, which is what you want because when they start talking to you about their passion, you can begin to listen and gain information about what is important to them.

Always keep your prospects/customers' interests first.

3. Know what sets them apart.

Are they collectors who specialize in a very rare form of antiques? If so, what is it? Find out what makes them different. What about their hobby or interest do they perceive makes them special?

Do you notice how this has nothing to do with business and everything to do with getting to know them as human beings? That's because selling is never about the product or service. It is always about people.

The more you can dig into getting to who they are and showing them that you care, the easier it will be to make them your customer. Not just once, but a life-long customer with the potential to bring you valuable leads and business opportunities for years to come.

If you remember nothing else in this book, remember this:

SELLING IS ALWAYS ABOUT PEOPLE, NOT THE PRODUCT OR SERVICE YOU ARE SELLING.

6 THE 70/20/10 RULE

The 70/20/10 Percent Rule should be the standard by which you conduct all marketing efforts. This includes online social media as well as face-to-face marketing.

- 70% of the time you should be talking about and/or posting information that is useful to your prospects and customers.
- 20% of the time you should be talking about and/or posting information that comes from other sources.
- 10% of the time you should be talking about and/or posting about you and your business.

So why do you think that the smallest percentage is designated to talking about your business? Is this the opposite of what you have been taught in the past or seen by others?

The reason is simple. People are wary of those who talk about themselves almost exclusively. It shows no consideration or thought for others and displays an intention of being self-absorbed.

Instead, when you offer free, useful information without any strings or expectations attached, you build trust with others. The vibe you put out conveys a sincere interest in helping others. That is what your customers want to feel. They want to know they can trust that you will see to their needs above your own.

This is the secret to marketing anything.

7 BRANDING

What is branding?

Branding is creating a memorable tag line or catch phrase that helps customers remember who you are. Branding is also using the same design on all of your marketing materials so that they are easy to identify when seen repeatedly. In other words, branding is differentiating yourself from others in your field.

Why Brand yourself?

From a customer's perspective, there are plenty of accountants to choose from. No one really knows how to distinguish one person from another and quite often a random pick is what customers will do based on their needs.

The good news is that you only have to do a little more than the rest of the accountants in your field to stand out and distinguish yourself.

It is still going to be a lot of work but the work isn't hard. It will need to be consistent and focused, though. Branding helps make it a lot easier to identify yourself from everyone else.

Golden arches.

Tissue to blow your nose.

"Give me a break, give me a break. Break me off a piece of that Kit Kat bar."

What do you think of when you read these? You think of the product that goes with it. McDonalds has the golden arches, you call a tissue to blow your nose a Kleenex and the jingle is obviously a Kit Kat candy bar.

This is branding.

It is important that you take time to establish what your tagline and mission statement will be. There are so many accountants I've seen that add a boring, uninspiring tagline to their marketing materials that say nothing of how they distinguish themselves from everyone else. It is obvious little thought went into it and I would argue that in some cases it may actually do more harm than good.

Your branding should align with your chosen specialty or niche. It should reflect your target audience and how you can help them.

8 TESTIMONIALS

Testimonials are wonderful little selling machines. They do a great job of convincing prospects to give your business a chance. They are outside sources that speak on your behalf, assuring customers that they will have a pleasant experience using you.

Why it is important to acquire testimonials?

Testimonials are statements made by previous customers that declare their experience with you was a positive one. Customers give you their permission to write what they have said and to use it as a marketing tool for your business. This means that they have "vouched" for you publicly.

People in general know this and that is why they pay closer attention when they see you have testimonials. It soothes many reservations they might have about buying from someone they don't know well.

The more testimonials you can gather over the course of your career, the more solid your business will seem to new customers. However, <u>NEVER EVER</u> falsify or make up testimonials. They should always come from real people and real sources.

How to get testimonials.

Keep your ears open when dealing with customers. They may give you a compliment or make a statement to someone about you in your presence. If it is a statement you can use, then ask them if you can quote them as a testimonial on your website and marketing materials. Always get their permission first.

Once a project is finished, ask them if they would write a testimonial for you. This is important so make this a habit. You can miss out on many opportunities to build great testimonials by being shy. Most people are happy to help you, especially if they felt they received a positive experience from you.

Do not underestimate the power of testimonials to your business. They are worth their weight in gold. It is a chance for others to speak about your business and a chance for you to show new customers your competence as a accountant business owner.

9 SUCCESS STORIES

Success stories are similar to testimonials, only longer. They explain a story or situation in which a customer used your products or services and had a positive outcome. Unlike testimonials, you can write these yourself as long as the events actually happened. If you are going to use a customer's name, you need to ask permission first, but you don't have to use their name. You can write a generalized story about a problem your customer had and how you helped them solve it.

Why it is important to have success stories?

Success stories show customers your method of how you solve problems. They show how you can help customers overcome their problems and achieve their goals. What you do is important and you should be proud to demonstrate the ways in which you can help your customers. Success stories are not boasting. When presented as a series of factual events, they can convey a powerful story for hiring you.

10 COLD CALLING

Oh boy. It's the dreaded cold calling discussion.

If you have ever held a sales job before, it is likely you have encountered the issue of cold calling.

It's miserable. It's torture. It's the worst part of marketing that everyone dreads.

What if I told you that cold calling can be fun? It can! When done correctly, you position yourself from feeling like a beggar with your hand out asking prospects for their time to hear your pitch to a position of empowerment where you are sharing powerful information with the prospect that they identify as valuable and useful.

There is no reason to fear cold calling. That is, when you know how to do it right. How many times have you received a telemarketing call and reacted with anger and annoyance?

Why?

Because you know what's coming. The pitch. They want something from you and you don't want to give it to them. You are annoyed because you don't really want to disappoint them and you resent them for putting you in that situation.

What if those telemarketers called you, not to ask you for something, but informed you that they were giving you something for free. I mean actually free. No strings attached. No sign up now for a free month. For real free. How would you feel then?

It is likely you would not feel resentful as they haven't asked you for anything in return. They haven't even asked you if you want the information, they told you they were sending it anyway. Would you still feel aggravated and resentful?

Cold calling can be fun when you see yourself as having the responsibility to educate the public on what they need to know when it comes to accountant. Even if they aren't in the market at the time, they will remember you when they are. You aren't holding your hand out begging them, you are Santa Clause in this scenario and your job is to give valuable informational nuggets without expecting anything in return.

Cold calling should never be used to sell a person on the phone or in an email. Its sole duty is to get an appointment to meet with prospects face-to-face (when possible). You should not try to vomit every bit of information on them about your services as fast as possible before they decide they don't want what you're selling.

All you are trying to do is introduce yourself and give them free information to help them. That's it. The Law of Reciprocity will do the heavy lifting. All you have to do is share the information.

11 BUILD RELATIONSHIPS

Building relationships is the heart of your marketing strategy. Marketing is all about how you make people feel. You have to convince them that you are sincere in your efforts to help them.

Start with your sphere of influence.

Friends, family, classmates, co-workers, acquaintances—all of these people are in your sphere of influence. They are people within your immediate circle whom you can reach out to and begin your marketing campaign.

Ask them about their lives without selling them.

The fastest way to lose your friends is to try selling them. The act comes across to them as being disrespectful. They feel that you have little respect for your friendship and will sell anyone. This is the worst way to get new business.

Instead, ask them about their lives. Pay attention to their responses. Ask them follow-up questions about themselves. Be present in your friendship with them. Actually care about them. Remember birthdays and anniversaries. Congratulate them on important events in their lives. Show you care about them.

It is your character as a friend that sells your business. Not trying to get them to do something for you. Care about them and they will care about you.

Stay consistent.

Marketing is a never-ending process. You should always be marketing yourself and your business. However, when you market by caring about others, it becomes not only unbelievably gratifying in your own life, but can pay off a thousand times over in the long run.

You must stay consistent for this to be successful. This doesn't mean you hound the same people week after week. It means you pick three new people each day and send them a personal email or phone call about how they are doing. Start a conversation with your Facebook friends. Follow up with them, ask them questions. They will follow the Law of Reciprocity and ask you how you are doing. That doesn't mean you start selling them. Yes, you can say that you are a accountant, but unless they start asking you specific questions, I wouldn't go into anything more than that.

Another way to keep conversations going is to offer free, valuable information related to your accountant business and post it to your social media sites. This should not just be about you, but should also be about local events and accountant related information. You could even offer accountant tips and tricks— anything that offers practical and useful information that most anyone can use.

Provide a resource of quality information consistently and people will see you as a source of credible information.

12 NETWORKING

The way you meet new customers is by getting out there and meeting new people. Sometimes this can mean meeting a lot of people. Some may enjoy this part of the business while others may dread it, but it is a necessary evil when building your business.

Always be open to meeting new contacts. Make sure you have a positive attitude and realize that meeting new people is an opportunity to help them and share your business. When you look at it from the perspective of helping people, you realize that what you have to offer is of great value for those needing your products and services. No longer are you perceived (or perceive yourself) as just another salesperson, but you are a teacher with a higher purpose of education people about your craft.

Attend community functions. Grab your calendar and open it to the beginning of next month. Go online and find your community's event calendar. This can be found either on the Chamber of Commerce website or your county's website. Take note of all the planned events. Choose those that you feel you would both enjoy and have the most opportunity to meet new people. Schedule it on your calendar and follow through by attending.

Try to plan as far ahead as you can and get it in your calendar. Make sure you list several opportunities in case you can't make a couple of them. The only reason you shouldn't attend those events you have chosen ahead of time is if there is an emergency. Don't let excuses convince you that you could just catch the next event. You never know who may be at that event and the opportunities you could miss.

Every new person you meet is a lead, a chance to build a new relationship. Follow-up is essential. It does you no good to meet new people if you don't continue to build a relationship with them. This could be as simple as taking their business card and looking them up on social media. Add them as a friend and then start commenting on their posts here and there. Not too much but just enough that they keep you in mind when they need you.

13 ONLINE PRESENCE

Regardless of your personal view about online social media, there is no denying that it is here to stay. If you are old school and prefer traditional methods of meeting people, there is nothing wrong with that. However, if you are not plugged in online, you are passing up half the business you could be getting by not being available in that medium.

The principles of marketing dictate that you go where the people are. That means if you have to learn how to build a Facebook page, then that is what you have to do. Consider it continuing education to benefit your business. Those who resist new ways to reach new customers will limit their own income.

Social media is a great way to spread valuable information and build relationships fast. Simple comments on other people's posts can leave a lasting impression on those you are trying to connect with. It only takes a few minutes a day to form the habit of connecting with others.

Make sure that your social media profiles reflect your professionalism. If you have a personal page already, then consider creating a professional page for your business.

Social media will only be as effective as you are engaged in it. Consistent updates are important to show others that you are a constant resource of new and valuable information.

14 CUSTOMER SERVICE

Provide superior customer service consistently. This is a non-negotiable rule. It should be your top priority to always provide excellent customer service. This means that you do everything you can do to provide the best experience for your customers.

This also means that you are always looking for new and improved ways to provide better customer service. What services are your competitors providing? How can you take that one step further? What ways can you create new concepts that make customer experiences better?

It is also important to become efficient in how to deal with unhappy customers. Knowing how to resolve problems is just as important as providing good service. Your goal is to keep your customers for the life of your career. You want them to return to you and refer others to you.

Do not confuse excellent customer service with allowing customers to walk all over you. That is not customer service. Make sure that you keep the value of your business apparent with customers. Too many free things can backfire on you. Some people will take advantage of kindness or perceived weakness, although most people will not. Be aware of when you need to set boundaries.

15 FOLLOW-UP

Follow-up can be just as important as making the sale because it's where future business comes from. It is also an opportunity to show customers that you care about them after the sale has completed. Thanking a customer shows that you find their business valuable to you, but also you find their relationship important as well.

There are several ideas you can come up with that will show your customers you appreciate their business. Even a series of follow-up phone calls two, six and twelve weeks out can do a lot to keep your customers happy. Remember that they want to know you care. Not just during the sale but after.

So many people forget to follow-up with their customers. In doing so, they forfeit an opportunity to get feedback on how they can improve their marketing efforts. You want to know what your customers think about your craft, and following up with them gives you the opportunity to know whether or not they will be a good referral source for you in the future.

16 REFERRALS

Many accountants are too shy to ask for referrals. Why? If you did a good job with your customers, why would you feel awkward asking for something they are probably happy to give you?

Asking for referrals is a prize opportunity to get warm leads. Customers want to help their friends and family and would be excited to refer someone they trusted and with whom they had a positive experience with.

Have confidence in your business and yourself to know that you deserve to ask for referrals. It's a chance to help more people and continue your excellent customer service.

Referrals also build confidence in customers. They are far more likely to take the referral from someone they know, so when you follow-up on referrals, realize that they tend to be more receptive than those you are cold calling.

Failure to ask for referrals is like leaving money on the table. Referrals aren't just about getting you new business, it's also about those who refer you. People love to be the hero in their own lives. Think how good you would make them look to their friends and family when you successfully help someone they care about.

17 SUBJECT MATTER EXPERT

One of the fastest ways to establish yourself as a credible source of accountant information is to position yourself as a subject matter expert. This means that you offer a consistent stream of helpful information available to the public. It also means that your business is out in front of the public.

Writing a book, posting consistent blog articles, and streaming tips on social media are all ways to establish yourself as an expert. Offering free public workshops and seminars is another great way to build a positive reputation. Utilizing local radio and television shows to get your face and name out there while handing out good information can also do a lot to gain free advertising for your business and increase your subject matter expert reputation.

Make sure that as your reputation within the community gathers momentum that the information you give is accurate, well-researched and based on factual data. It is not acceptable to simply pass on information from sources that have not been verified. It takes a lot of effort to build a positive reputation and almost no effort to have that reputation destroyed by bad information.

Every piece of advice you give should be accurate and well thought out.

18 STEP-BY-STEP MARKETING PLAN

Here is a list of marketing steps that you should implement immediately. Take a couple and master them before taking on anymore. Make each task a habit, something you do on a daily, weekly or monthly basis. Track your results consciously so that you can see how each strategy is working for your business.

1. Blog useful information consistently and link to social media. Write or hire a copywriter to write blog posts on your website (you should have a website). Link every post on every social media site- Facebook, Twitter, Pinterest, Instagram, etc.

2. Contact three friends per day on social media and catch up. These are current friends. Send them a private message asking them how they are doing. Follow up and engage them in a conversation. Do not sell them on your products or services.

3. Facebook friend three new people every day. Don't just click the "add friend" button. Send them a short, quick private message commenting on why you want to add them as a friend.

4. Join as many niche groups as possible. This includes your hobbies and interest groups. Engage by complimenting and commenting on other people's posts. Do not try to sell them on your product or services. Build relationships on the basis of your mutual interest.

5. Find forum groups and engage. Engage in conversations and debates but avoid topics of politics and religion. Keep your engagements professional.

6. Put your information in your signature line. This is an opportunity to quietly advertise so use it. Include your contact information and your branding tagline and/or mission statement.

7. Go to as many networking events as possible. Your goal is to meet new people and ask them about their interests and business. Collect business cards and social media contacts. Follow-up with them on social media and keep in contact to build a relationship.

8. Join or form a weekly or monthly group workshop. If there is an existing group that aligns with your accountant business, then join it. If there isn't one, then form one. This is an excellent way to gain leads and build trust by providing free information.

9. Offer free workshops at local library or recreation center. Coordinate an ongoing workshop and advertise to the public. Gather leads and teach accountant classes.

10. Follow-up with personal touches, going above and beyond, postcards, letters, etc. Make this a consistent habit before, during and after each contact with customers. Let them know you have their interests in mind and as a priority.

11. Offer a free online course. There are websites like Udemy that allow you to create an entire online course. You can charge for it or offer it for free. Make a accountant 101 course and offer it for free. Link it to all social media and put it on your website. Advertise it consistently in your emails to your subscription list.

12. Offer a free giveaway consultation or prize. People like free stuff. Create a prize of value and run a contest on social media to offer it for free. This will give you leads.

13. Submit press releases to media. I would hire a copywriter to write an effective press release about something that is happening in your business. If you are going to try to do this yourself, then remember that a press release should be written from the perspective of the media in mind. This means that they are always looking for interesting stories to tell the public. Write your press release in a way that is a factual and interesting story that the public would like to know more about. This is one of the best and free ways to advertise your business when done correctly.

14. Volunteer at a local charity and offer to donate a portion of the proceeds. Your first intention should be to help others. Volunteering does wonders for the soul. It also can do wonders for your business. When you are involved in charities and efforts in helping others, you reinforce yourself as someone who puts the needs of others first.

15. Initiate monthly themes that engage your audience. You can make this as fun as you want. The holidays are a great time to feature themed blog posts and social media posts. Offer tips, tricks and techniques that customers can use. Implement a giveaway in line with that month's theme.

16. Offer a free report or eBook as a way to build your mailing list. Writing a book is one of the fastest ways to present yourself as a subject-matter expert. Hire a copywriter or write the book yourself. Then offer it for free when people sign up for your subscription list.

17. Send frequent emails to your list with useful information. Utilize your email list regularly. Find a comfortable middle ground on the frequency of emails. Too much and you will risk losing your audience, too few and you risk losing your audience. One email a week to your list filled with several articles of useful information, event information and new promotions should suffice.

18. Regularly cold call new contacts. Make it part of your weekly to-do items to cold call a certain number of new contacts. You can also email them but make sure that each email is sent individually and use their name in the subject line and as the greeting. The more personal you make it, the more likely they are to open it. Try to make 10-20 cold calls per day.

19. Gather testimonials. At the end of each business deal ask your customer for a testimonial. Provide an email or a statement where they agree to let you use their testimonial in your marketing efforts.

20. Ask for referrals. This should also be a standard practice at the end of each deal with your customer. Try to get at least three referrals and make sure to follow up with each of them.

21. Speak at schools, colleges, career days, etc. This is part of getting your name well-known in the community. Bring flyers, brochures, business cards or postcards with you to pass out. Make sure you give them your contact information including social media information.

22. Get your face and name out in the community as often as possible. Networking at community functions, teaching, speaking at public events—anything you can do to get out there and meet as many people as possible.

23. Create a weekly podcast show. This can be a short 5-10 minute podcast where you share the highlights of the week in current events and how it relates to your accountant business.

24. Be a guest on a local radio show. Again, you are there to share useful, valuable information. Try to get a regular spot and offer to have guests call in with their questions so you can answer them on the air.

25. Be a guest on a local morning T.V. show. Same principle as the local radio show. It will get your name and face out there while you offer information to the community.

26. Start your own YouTube channel. Offer free and valuable information in short video segments. Link these videos to your website and social media platforms.

27. Have Q&A sessions on Twitter. Make yourself available once a week or twice a month to take accountant questions from your followers.

28. Post your listings to Pinterest, Instagram, Facebook, YouTube, and Twitter. Use as many pictures as possible. Make your accountant descriptions creative, mysterious and fun.

29. Hire an assistant. If you are doing all or most of these things, you may find that in order to meet the demand of maintaining your marketing efforts you will need to hire an assistant who can do some of these tasks for you and keep your organized and focused.

30. Hire a marketing copywriter. If writing and putting together compelling marketing articles is not your strong suit, do not do what everyone else does and try to do it yourself. You will only waste your time and your product will be less than it could be. Instead, invest in a quality copywriter who has experience writing in a way that compel people to take action. In the long run it will actually save you time and money.

31. Advertise in your niche areas. Do not advertise in all the same ways and in all the same places as every other accountant.

Instead, keep to your niche and advertise there. Stay close to your niche and you will often find you are the only accountant around.

32. Offer a resource guide. Create a guide that gives customers great information about what to look for when buying your product or service. Post it on your website and link it to all your social media sites.

There you have it!

Sixteen marketing strategies to change the face of your accountant business and 32 step-by-step tasks to get you started on effectively marketing your business. These strategies can be applied to most every form of business. It can also be applied to forming relationships in almost every setting.

Selling and marketing is always about people. When you know how to build relationships with others, the money will always follow.

Happy marketing!

THANK YOU

Before you go, I would just like to say "THANK YOU" for purchasing my book. There are many books out there but you took a chance on mine. So, a big thank you for reading it all the way to the end.

If you liked what you have read, then please leave a review on Amazon. This feedback will help me continue to write the kind of books you enjoy.

www.ingramcontent.com/pod-product-compliance
Lightning Source LLC
Chambersburg PA
CBHW071829200526
45169CB00018B/1300